BOOKS BY MARVIN BELL

POETRY

*Drawn by Stones, by Earth, by Things that Have
Been in the Fire*　1984
These Green-Going-to-Yellow　1981
Stars Which See, Stars Which Do Not See　1977
Residue of Song　1974
The Escape into You　1971
A Probable Volume of Dreams　1969

LIMITED EDITIONS

Woo Havoc (pamphlet)　1971
Things We Dreamt We Died For　1966
Poems for Nathan and Saul (pamphlet)　1966

POETRY COLLABORATIONS

Segues: A Correspondence in Poetry (with William Stafford)　1983

PROSE

Old Snow Just Melting: Essays and Interviews　1983

Drawn by Stones, by Earth, by Things that Have Been in the Fire

Drawn by Stones, by Earth, by Things that Have Been in the Fire

POEMS BY

Marvin Bell

ATHENEUM

NEW YORK

1984

Grateful acknowledgment is made to the editors of the following periodicals in which these poems previously appeared:

THE AMERICAN POETRY REVIEW: *Against Stuff, Days of Time, The Facts of Life, How I Got the Words, In, In Those Days, Leaving a Resort Town, Questions to Answers, To Be, A True Story* and *A Young Woman Sunning in the Nude.*
THE AMICUS JOURNAL: *The Stones.*
ANTAEUS: *They* and *Youth.*
THE ANTIOCH REVIEW: *The White Pony* (under the title *In Two Parts*).
THE ATLANTIC MONTHLY: *Banyan Tree Before the Civic Center, Honolulu, Jane Was with Me* and *White Clover.*
THE MISSOURI REVIEW: *Shoulders of Tropical Rain.*
NEW ENGLAND REVIEW AND BREAD LOAF QUARTERLY: *Starfish.*
THE NEW YORKER: *Drawn by Stones, by Earth, by Things that Have Been in the Fire, The Nest* and *Unless It Was Courage.*
THE PARIS REVIEW: *Felt but Not Touched.*
POETRY: *Draft Age.*
SONORA REVIEW: *Personal Reasons* and *Three Implements.*
TRIQUARTERLY: *Chicago, 1959* and *Instructions to Be Left Behind.*
THE VIRGINIA QUARTERLY REVIEW: *One of the Animals, Three Letters, Trees as Standing for Something* and *Who & Where.*

Some of these poems are dedicated, as follows: "Drawn by Stones, by Earth, by Things that Have Been in the Fire," to Frank and Carole DiGangi; "Jane Was with Me," to Jane Cooper; and "A Young Woman Sunning in the Nude" to Gregory Orr.

Library of Congress catalog card number 83-72998
ISBN 0-689-11466-4 (clothbound)
*   0-689-11467-2 (paperback)*
Published simultaneously in Canada by McClelland and Stewart Ltd.
Composed and printed by Heritage Printers, Charlotte, North Carolina
Bound by The Delmar Company, Charlotte, North Carolina
Designed by Harry Ford
First Edition

To my wife, Dorothy,
and my sons, Nathan and Jason

CONTENTS

Drawn by Stones,
by Earth, by Things
that Have Been in
the Fire

Youth

Begins again in a kiss, in a passionate word,
begins where lazy fingers again feel suddenly
the surface of an ordinary thing—
in a gesture larger than anything a person can say,
and all this in a moment smaller than a second,
in a look that passes, in the flicker of a star,
as in between two ratchetings of a turning wheel.

How fat the English sparrows had become!
How limp the lovebirds seemed in their slow movements!
They say that, in winter, ice will warm the water
beneath it, but people will tell you anything.
There are people anxious to tell you you are losing
your hair, your mind, your slender disposition
and good luck, failing to live up to a promise

you never made. I remember the look of the fields
the day I came flying home from beautiful Elsewhere
to the racks of sunstruck corn suffering summer.
How beautiful were these rediscovered rectangles
beneath our wings, down there dumb to intention
in the black truth of an indifferent earth.
I had been away, and darkly thought again of you.

Drawn by Stones, by Earth, by Things
that Have Been in the Fire

I can tell you about this because I have held in my hand
the little potter's sponge called an "elephant ear."
Naturally, it's only a tiny version of an ear,
but it's the thing you want to pick up out of the toolbox
when you wander into the deserted ceramics shop
down the street from the cave where the fortune-teller works.
Drawn by stones, by earth, by things that have been in the fire.

The elephant ear listens to the side of the vase
as it is pulled upwards from a dome of muddy clay.
The ear listens to the outside wall of the pot
and the hand listens to the inside wall of the pot,
and between them a city rises out of dirt and water.
Inside this city live the remains of animals,
animals who prepared for two hundred years to be clay.

Rodents make clay, and men wearing spectacles make clay,
though the papers they were signing go up in flames
and nothing more is known of these long documents
except by those angels who divine in our ashes.
Kings and queens of the jungle make clay
and royalty and politicians make clay although
their innocence stays with their clothes until unravelled.

There is a lost soldier in every ceramic bowl.
The face on the dinner plate breaks when the dish does
and lies for centuries unassembled in the soil.
These things that have the right substance to begin with,
put into the fire at temperatures that melt glass,
keep their fingerprints forever, it is said,
like inky sponges that walk away in the deep water.

4

The White Pony

1

Where is the book in which I wished to look again?
There on page two hundred and seventy-seven,
a poet of indescribable lightness,
a poet who could speak with birds and trees,
likened herself to a flower—revealing
only that the flower was yellow,
revealing neither its name nor location,
nor the depth and length of its knowledge.
Since, I have been everywhere in search of it.
Not in books only, but deep in alleys and woods,
where I see that I am neither tree nor city
weed, growing in concrete, nor any flower.
Perhaps if I choose for myself the right color,
I might become like all objects given that color,
and I myself might impart my color
to each dimension, and in all directions.
I shall be white, the white of all colors at once,
the white behind yellow, beneath the sky,
at the edge of an eye, or a fingernail or toenail,
the white where no letters appear on the page,
the white that surrounds the voice that says,
"I am thinner than a yellow flower."

2

And now I find it again. Loafing
in the bath, I see that on this page
the flower is named by a conscientious editor.
A chrysanthemum. Favorite of a friend.
I find that I am not pleased to be informed.
It is as though I could see in the air about me
a road for the wind, or in the forest
a hook to pull the trees up to their full height.
I did not wish to know so much.

Let her be just a chrysanthemum for the knowing.
I believe she is also the slenderness of yellow,
and moves like a curtain at an open window
and speaks with the owl in the daytime.
I believe she could not have written one such line
and lived as I see some others of my time living—
so big and proud they are, and keep records.
She who is the yellow of a flower in the sun
must touch the white wastes, the accumulations.
And she is thin, who can bow low.

Trees as Standing for Something

1

More and more it seems I am happy with trees
and the light touch of exhausted morning.
I wake happy with her soft breath on my neck.
I wake happy but I am happier yet.
For my loves are like the leaves in summer.
But oh!, when they fall, and I wake with a start,
will I feel the sting of betrayal and ask, What is this
love, if it has to end, even in death,
or if one might lose it even during a life?
Who will care for such a thing?
Better to cut it down where it stands.
Better to burn it, and to burn with it,
than to turn around to see one's favorite gone.

2

It began when they cut down the elm and I let them.
When the corkscrew willow withered and I said nothing.
Then when the soft maple began to blow apart,
when the apple tree succumbed to poison,
the pine to a matrix of bugs, the oak to age,
it was my own limbs that were torn off, or so it seemed,
and my love, which had lived through many storms,
died, again and again. Again and again, it perished.
What was I to say then but Oh, Oh, Oh, Oh, Oh!
Now you see a man at peace, happy and happier yet,
with her breath on the back of his neck in the morning,
and of course you assume it must always have been this way.
But what was I to say, then and now, but Oh! and Oh! Oh!

Instructions to Be Left Behind

I've included this letter in the group
to be put into the cigar box—the one
with the rubber band around it you will find
sometime later. I thought you might
like to have an example of the way in which
some writing works. I may not say anything
very important or phrase things just-so,
but I think you will pay attention anyway
because it matters to you—I'm sure it does,
no one was ever more loved than I was.

What I'm saying is, your deep attention
made things matter—made art,
made science and business
raised to the power of goodness, and sport
likewise raised a level beyond.
I am not attaching to this a photograph
though no doubt you have in your mind's eye
a clear image of me in several expressions
and at several ages all at once—which is
the great work of imagery beyond the merely
illustrative. Should I stop here for a moment?

These markings, transliterations though they are
from prints of fingers, and they from heart
and throat and corridors the mind guards,
are making up again in you the one me
that otherwise would not survive that manyness
daisies proclaim and the rain sings much of.
Because I love you, I can almost imagine
the eye for detail with which you remember
my face in places indoors and out and far-flung,
and you have only to look upwards to see

in the plainest cloud the clearest lines
and in the flattest field your green instructions.

Shall I rest a moment in green instructions?
Writing is all and everything, when you care.
The kind of writing that grabs your lapels
and shakes you—that's for when you don't care
or even pay attention. This isn't that kind.
While you are paying your close kind of attention,
I might be writing the sort of thing you think
will last—as it is happening, now, for you.
While I was here to want this, I wanted it,
and now that I am your wanting me to be myself
again, I think myself right up into being
all that you (and I too) wanted me to be: You.

Leaving a Resort Town

Get away, said something that wasn't
human, and I took a fix on distance.
Sometimes when I see what became
of those breakers—low and thin now
in the parking lot, or soggy underfoot
where the yard slants toward the creek—
and the wind—sometimes you have to
watch the trees to see it—
I know what spoke.

At home, here, they say
sink, *sink*, not that other thing;
and *listen*, *listen*, not what others said.
Any sea is a farm, and you can hum
and walk until, far, you hear yourself
again. Land: no edge, no end.
Suppose you always got where you were going.

Who & Where

1

Where I live, it's a long uphill to
the Great Divide where larger men crossed
a streak in the land rivers know.
Somewhere else there may be gold in the trees
or dollars in the view. Here, we may be
nowhere ourselves but everywhere
on the way—so stop sometimes. We've eats,
nights, scars on the land, earth

you can pick up and squeeze,
the obvious. Sometimes we leave in
a line of dirt in a crack of skin.
If you drive past, you may see strange creatures
crossing the land, leaving behind them
heaps, bales, piles, clumps. And in the land:
supply lines, lost fingers, implements
left to rust where nothing now will grow.

2

Who I am is a short person with small feet
and fingers. When the hill is snowy,
I have to walk on the grass, and this gives
me a different viewpoint and wet shoes.
I see writers grow huge
in their writings. I get smaller yet,
so small that sometimes a tree is more
than I can look up to. I am down here with
all the other tiny, weak things. Sure,
once in a while I pull myself up
to assert something to the air, but oftener
I look for what was lost in the weeds.
The Gods drink nectar, I drink fruit juice.
All my life, people have told me,

"You are big, or will be." But I'm small.
I am not at the center of the circle.
I am not part of the ring. Like you,
I am not the core, the dark star or the lit star.
I take a step. The wind takes a step.
I take a drink of water. The earth swallows.
I just live here—like you, like you, like you.

Against Stuff

What is it that I should be
to be able to look out at night beyond
whatever intrudes
and see there, undistracted by sunlight
on the hard edges of machines
or shining out from the glassy eyeballs
of men and women going to work,—
see there what I need, or you need, or god
forbid the world
will have been said to have needed
if anyone survives
the coming instantaneous flaming
of all books and other records, people
and animals and vegetation
and machines which could not suffer
that much light at one time?

I do not believe for a moment that the last
poet in the last standing building
while the world splits up and caves inward
like the crust of a rich cake
will be trying to make a line come out right;
nor does it seem remotely possible
to anyone who believes, as I do,
that those standards and agreements
which will have brought us
our end, as well as any last
prospecting of the future, any last words,
could possibly be right;
and, if we are shortly to find ourselves
without beast, field or flower,
is it not right that we now prepare
by removing them from our poetry?

The beauty that goes up in flame
is touchable beauty—the beauty of things
in light; of all manner of representing
people, mouths open or closed forever;
and of beauty known by its shape
in the dark, or by whatever hides and reveals it—
beauty received, registered,
the object of study, talent and abandon.
But still there is another beauty
known to us by such measures as "yesterday,"
"tomorrow," "at a distance," or
"inextricable and transcendent," and which
we cannot be, but can only conceive
and cause. Will we, always?
I suggest, knowing that every form and habit
has been described, that the forms are wrong,

the habits harmful, and the objects too many.
If I can see, it is only because it is dark.

Felt but Not Touched
— Seattle

That light behind the Olympics at supper hour—
it takes a sky of clouds from here to there
to spot the sun, seam and snow just right.
That pulsating light, a sizable incandescence
out of the grayness—that's the wing or tail of a plane.
The roundness of things—that's knowledge, a new way
to touch it here. (On the plains, we see Earth curve,
and I have seen the sun melt into the ocean elsewhere
and then call a color or two it left behind down.)

Then it is dark. The great streak of sunlight
that showed our side of snowy peaks has gone ahead.
Those bumps on the holly tree we passed
getting home for the late afternoon view from upstairs—
next to them, some smaller trees and a porch,
and next to that the streaky windows and then
the whole household getting ready to make the break
into spring—and sometimes in late winter we can't
sit still for connecting time at both ends.

If anything we do or don't will keep the world
for others, it will need such distant knowledge—beyond
experience, provable by ones, felt but not touched.
As we watch the light in the distance move on and around,
and the air at mountain height take up the cause of snow,
all that is beneath us that is not light has stopped.

Questions to Answers

For my unique voice,
for my solitary vision,
I was given the song of a bird
outside my window
and all of the songs that answered
to it.
For my way with words,
for my unusual behavior, listen,
I was given an essence of chocolate
which only made me desire
all other chocolates.
For my individual grief,
for my perfect isolation,
I was given maps to mass graves
on every continent
and still for my feet I was given shoes
and for my hands gloves in winter
and now if I ask
whose shoes otherwise and whose
gloves if not mine
I offend those who liked my poems
for a while.
And this is why I have come to believe
that there are, to my questions,
answers
after all.

How I Got the Words

I was in Hawaii, but the letter
had come from Alaska. I hadn't read it
when a breeze lifted it out the open louvres
of what I called "my office"
and there it proceeded like a kite or light
hat rocking to one side and then the other
looking both ways for a landing
before swooping one way only for earth.
It was gone. I stood on the ground
and tried to guess. Vacancies everywhere.
So I let a second paper go
through the slot and into the hand of the wind
which here comes a thousand miles
and takes away the sucking part of the heat—
which now I see again carries your letter,
written on two sides, with more compassion
than any poor bodied brain with heart
can hope to heaven for,
and *cradles* it down and down to where
such gentleness will not protect it longer,
and then gives it an alley of air
such as the sleekest aircraft might require
to down itself down the very arc of the earth.
I followed to your letter the blank page
which landed exactly next to it
by every physical and mental measure
only as you had filled your page to me
by putting words next to silence,
and the sound of hundreds of lungs
to bear it away, if one has friends.

Draft Age

You probably thought you were going to go through life
with red eyes and sore knees, with elbows
worn down from shoving and making room, and a cut lip.
You probably didn't believe you would see adulthood
after the bullies, the grownups' supper talk
about "conditions" in the world, and the salient fact
that no one saw what you saw in the clouds.

It's always difficult when they stop humoring you
and start using real bullets: time to wear
a helmet—a plastic liner goes inside a steel pot
and up inside the webbing goes the most important
thing: toilet paper, wads and wads of the stuff.
The mess kit goes inside your shirt to ward off
pains in the stomach. Like an aluminum death-rattle.

You probably thought you were going to go through life
wounded, fearful, always watching your step
as in school, or afterwards retreating through alleys.
Little did you realize, good student though you were,
that the real tests lay elsewhere in places
left out of your history books, where when
you were being victimized, great reversals were in store.

A True Story

One afternoon in my room
in Rome,
I found, wedged
next to the wheel of a wardrobe,
so far under
no maid's broom could touch it,
a pouch made from a sock.
Inside were diamonds
in several sizes. Spread on the carpet,
they caught in my throat.
I knew that, from that moment on,
I would never answer the door.
All of my holiday
would be a preparation
for leaving. First,
I would have to leave the hotel,
probably the city.
I knew someone I could trust
and another with nerve.
She would carry home
half of them, perhaps in her underwear,
if it was not of the kind
customs officers like to touch.
I would carry the others
by way of Zurich,
stopping to purchase
eucalyptus cigarettes, chocolates
and a modest music box
with its insides exposed.
After that, who knows?
Keep them for years?
Lug them into the shade and sell cheap?
A trip to a third country?
A middleman?

A True Story

So long as I didn't look up,
there with the stones before me
in the old room in the old city—
where embellishment of every fixture
and centuries of detail
took precedence
over every consideration
of light, air or space—
so long as I did not look up
to my suspicion,
I held the endless light of a fortune
and the course of a lifetime.

In retrospect, it was entirely appropriate
that my diamonds
were the ordinary pieces
of a chandelier, one string of which
had been pulled down
by a previous tenant of room three,
perhaps in a fit of ecstacy,
For I found, also—a diamond-
shaped third of its cover
hanging down from behind the wardrobe,
face to the wall—
the current issue of one of those men's
monthlies in which half-
nude women, glossy with wealth,
ooze to escape
from their lingerie.
And in the single page in its center,
someone had held his favorite
long enough to make love.
The pages were stuck together elsewhere also,
in no pattern,

and the articles on clothing and manners
left untouched.

So this was no ordinary hotel room,
or the most ordinary of all!
Men had come here many times no doubt
to make love by themselves.
But now
it was also a place of hidden treasure.
The rush of wealth and dark promise
I took from that room
I also put back. And so too everyone
who, when in Rome,
will do what the Romans do.

Jane Was with Me

Jane was with me
the day the rain dropped a squirrel *like that.*
An upside-down embrace,
a conical explosion from the sky,
a thick flowering of sudden water—
whatever it was,
the way it happened is
that first the trees grew a little,
and then they played music
and breathed songs and applauded themselves,
and that made the squirrel
surrender to nothing but the beauty
of a wet tree
about to shake its upper body like the devil.
And of course, of course,
he went out on that tree just as far as he could
when things were not so beautiful
and that was it: hard onto the roof of our car
before he could set his toes.

The flat whack of the body.
He lay in the street breathing and bleeding
until I could get back,
and then he looked me in the eye exactly.
Pasted to the concrete by his guts,
he couldn't lift, or leave, or live.
And so I brought the car and put its right tire
across his head. If in between
the life part and the death part,
there is another part,
a time of near-death,
we have come to know its length and its look
exactly—in this life always near death.
But there's something else.

Jane was with me.
After the rain, the trees were prettier yet.
And if I were a small animal with a wide tail,
I would trust them too. Especially
if Jane were with me.

White Clover

Once when the moon was out about three-quarters
and the fireflies who are the stars
of backyards
were out about three-quarters
and about three-fourths of all the lights
in the neighborhood
were on because people can be at home,
I took a not so innocent walk
out among the lawns,
navigating by the light of lights,
and there there were many hundreds of moons
on the lawns
where before there was only polite grass.
These were moons on long stems,
their long stems giving their greenness
to the center of each flower
and the light giving its whiteness to the tops
of the petals. I could say
it was light from stars
touched the tops of flowers and no doubt
something heavenly reaches what grows outdoors
and the heads of men who go hatless,
but I like to think we have a world
right here, and a life
that isn't death. So I don't say it's better
to be right here. I say this is where
many hundreds of core-green moons
gigantic to my eye
rose because men and women had sown green grass,
and flowered to my eye in man-made light,
and to some would be as fire in the body
and to others a light in the mind
over all their property.

Three Letters

Dear ――――――,

I am green, and I may well misunderstand your words, as even now I cannot read the precise condensations of the rain upon the outside of the thick glass of a recessed window on the fourth floor where I write this. Through the gray slats of window blinds, they line up like hieroglyphics, and I am as certain that I do not think correctly about this as I am that they should always appear to me to be amorphous cartoons squeezed from the weather unless I take steps. . . .

And so I might crack my fist against the glass, not changing a line of that watery writing which maintains its distance and temperature, but, in the pain and insanity with which I think of my battered hand, comes to be, in a life which has sides, the other side.

I detest the way that life is used as a metaphor for death, which only gives us death as a metaphor for life. I would rather have this sense of the other side, the condensed version, the utterly unreachable. For if I break through this window to take possession of what is on its other side, what will be left?

Only everything.

Dear ——————,

Today, when I pulled on a rope to open the blinds, the day was bright with light clouds like those which surround the peaks of the world's tallest mountains. And now the air is moving around enough to bend the tops of trees. An altogether satisfactory amalgam of wishes as portrayed in pictures and talk.

Behind a choppy cluster of full trees which ends my view in one direction within a hundred yards, there sits a small chapel rarely used now. Almost no one married in it is still married. It's not cursed. It is just very ordinary.

Others are bigger or smaller and known for it.

The chapel is open today. A ceremony for a woman who, it is said, died in Ireland, who once wore her hair long enough to touch the floor when she bowed, and who danced in circles of head and hair until the force of it flung her from this town and out of mind.

No doubt she thought she was a failure. Most businessmen, most scientists, and everyone in the arts thinks they are. I think she intended to live longer. I do. I know more and more people who are dead, which doesn't make them live. And I won't tell you how to say the end of that sentence. The mind can make all sounds at once.

The mind, starting from nothing but the privilege of darkness . . .

The mind, pulp and sinew, is destined never to complete a thought. As a life is destined to stop short, even if you live to be a hundred. In deception and pride, we have manufactured things to call complete. We are ourselves pieces of something, I am sure, but it would take the thinking of light itself to know what.

You wanted only to know how the river runs here, where the swords are among the trees, why the yellow flower is heading for the clouds, and maybe the attitude of the grass where some of the mourners are walking slowly towards the chapel, hands hanging heavily, rolling their steps so as to walk even more quietly. And I, I wanted to think about how time stops.

They are all in the chapel now, and the door closed.

Dear —————————,

Your very friendliness is a problem when we come to speak about feelings, so that sometimes we hurry into love-making so that we might not suffer any longer the slight feeling of mere happiness.

We want someone to be watching when we do these things that might kill us. We can only see ourselves in the other's face. Not in the eyes only but in the mouth and cheeks. Is the mouth held open and sounds pushed up from stomach and bowels held caught at the top of the throat? Then someone must be reaching deeper to grab and pull out those sounds. Does the mouth contort and the teeth come forward? Then great labors are taking place to open up the body. Do the eyes slam shut? Then you and she are nothing, a long explosion seen and heard by no one, a triumph without beauty or ugliness, in which the smallest grain of feeling punctures the skin like one of those jacketed bullets which penetrates an armored vehicle of war and slams about inside, chewing up metal and skin until it stops spinning and drops.

Later, a door or hatch may open and a soldier appear seemingly undamaged and fall out as if unable to work his legs. Right now, it appears that no one has been left alive.

One of the Animals

Why does a dog get sick?
—You tell me.

What does he do about it?
—You tell me.

Does it make a difference?
—You tell me.

Does he live or die?
—You tell me.

Does it make a difference?
—That one I know.

Does it prepare you?
—That one I know too.

Will we know what to do?
—You tell me.

Three Implements

Sugar Hammer

It is not necessary to describe such things as a sugar hammer. It is enough to realize that the sweetest things in the world, from the lowliest crystals aspiring to be rock candy up to the entire substance of an intimate group of ladies and gentlemen, chatting on the highly varnished deck of a pleasure boat as it takes them from A to B, summed up in the shimmering river and the sherry in their glasses, are not here for us to sample without battering, wrenching and the daily exhaustion of half our gain in the effort itself. Throwaways—poisoned, broken, inaccessible, unknown secrets of worms and mold. Hence, the sugar hammer is half cleaver.

Three Implements

Tortilla Press (Guanajuato)

In the market of the city of the dead
preserved for display,
I paid a squatting lump of old clothing a pittance
for my lunch.
I didn't die. There must be nourishment in the air
in the village in the hills.
There, no one eats much.
The earth is their floor and they pray.
The women put two wooden blocks face to face
and squeeze them
to make their daily bread.
An old woman will make a few to sell.
From a sack, from a moving hovel of rags, from a long life,
the warm food is offered
for practically nothing. A few cents. Nothing.
And always the warmth.
Then
the old women are gone from the market by siesta.
They cannot make tortillas by the loaf.
It is always one thing after another.

Pasta Shears

Wide-bladed pasta shears, you would make a miserable job of a haircut and fail utterly at trousers or paper dolls. Like all scissors, you talk talk talk and eat eat eat. Someone must be cooking a lot of spaghetti! But forgive me if I poke fun. I have seen the famous rivers of Rome and Paris where one finds on the banks in the mornings the soggy remains of love and the emptied vessels of spirits. Things severed there—a sudden loss of feeling after the explosion of romance, or the onset of a chill when the liquor has run out—will never again be whole. What silent rite is practiced by those who wield scissors? It might not do to know. For if pasta could speak . . . , or beans . . . , or cloth or paper. . . , or those animals who make such a racket in the slaughterhouses. . . , or men and women who have so many objects of use and so many uses for each. . .

Chicago, 1959

That was the time when photography approached
the ability of painting to make personal statements—
which Emerson had doubted. The same people
who had worn suspenders to bed for a hundred years
now believed that God was in Lake Michigan
and were shocked to see Harry Callahan's "Eleanor"
rising from the Lake like the Godhead itself
arrayed in light. In his photos of family,
unposed nudes blackened the eye of conventional
beauty, and his pictures of single reeds scratched
the surface of eyeballs glazed by years of postcards.

As always, there were wind and payoffs and butchering,
but also there were Siskind's South Side photos
of evidence of man: his large format camera
found faces in pavement and design in peeling
billboards and pieces of string and a lost glove
where the artist saw a symbol of leftover need.
The students of Siskind and Callahan clustered
at the Institute of Design, dreamless and persistent:
Rowinski, Galarneau, Swedlund, Jachna—
they were all bones and light and chemicals.
It was Postwar and, as it turned out, Prewar.

None of us knew that the sky had been getting lower
and soon the earth would disgorge forests of Vietnamese,
easily reachable by bombers and combat photographers.
The dark flow of images, once begun,
did not stop with unknown shapes in the mind
but crossed the barbed wire and stepped on the mines
that make pieces of flesh without light. If only
someone had thought to cover the shutter with a hat.
Chicago, you were the victim of a national truth.
To me, the best of you lies somewhere in the salvage
with the murdered door hinges of dead Hyde Park.

They

My destiny has been to prune one tree
to make it look more and more common.
Friends, I am still at it.

It has been suggested, knowing I plan a tattoo,
that I permit myself to be tattooed all over
and become, myself, a tree. Stick my arms out.

But that wouldn't be me. Nor would there be,
afterwards, as there is now,
the object of my desire

in the form of my desire unveiling.
What do they think this is all about?
Nothing was known before I came to know it.

The purpose of a tree is that I have given it:
to be the sane result of chaos,
to be so completely known it may be overlooked.

The Stones

One night in my room
many stones brought together over the years,
each bearing the gouges and pinpricks
of sea and shore life,
and each weighted according to the sea
which first chisels a slate
and then washes it and later writes on it
with an eraser—
these stones, large and small, flat,
rounded, conical, shapely or rough-hewn,
discussed their origins,
and then got around to me. One of them,
the white one full of holes
that wipes off on your hands, said
that he thinks I carry much sadness,
the weight of a heart full of stones,
and that I bring back these others
so that I might live among the obvious
heaviness of the world.
But another said that I carried him
six months in Spain
in a pants pocket and lifted him out
each night to place on the dresser,
and although he is small and flat,
like a planet seen from the moon,
I often held him up to the light,
and this is because I am able to lift
the earth itself. And isn't this
happiness? But a third stone spoke
from where it stood atop papers
and accused me of trying to manage
the entire world, which for the most part
is neither myself nor not myself,
and is also the air around the rim

of a moving wheel, the space beyond Space,
the water within water,
and the weight within the stone.
Then they all asked what right had I
to be happy or unhappy,
when the language of stones
was no different
from the language of a white lump of dung
among the excellent vegetables.

Personal Reasons

Your hair—short, long; stars, a bed
under stars, moon; your stars, your moon,
your embrace, your circumstances, my
buttons, your earrings; your collections
of moonlight in darkened rooms—let it all
fall when it will: so surrounded are we
already by all that we have lost
to each other, we could be god and goddess,
we could be grass and sky, flower and tree,
two of anything in romantic proximity. But
we are—that's it—one man and one woman,
alike we choose to believe. But it
(you and me) wasn't always that way,
or not so very much that very way—us.

A Young Woman Sunning in the Nude

I didn't think she had put herself out
for me, not for me,
and certainly she hadn't laid herself down
on a long chair by the water side
of the Hotel Dubrovnik
for the others, who stood about her
in ties and jackets, in gowns and heels,
all without looking.
I think she was oblivious to everything
but the music she had stuck in her ears
and the sun, which each day
defeats the government and burns off the night.
I think she hadn't had a thought in the shade
for many years. We got in her light,
my friend and I,
when we came waterside in the old man's boat,
stamping up onto the boards.
Everything stopped when she sat up. We too.
But I don't think her hello meant more
than hello, then or now. She was there for
someone she would meet after dark,
someone for whom she would dress up.
For the rest of us, nothing
would do. And we, we
had to close our eyes to see her after that.
Uplifted and dismayed,
I was like a man who holds an open umbrella
in such perfect weather as brings us
into the light and a slight smell of celery.

Banyan Tree Before the Civic Center, Honolulu

Hairy
like a man wearing a dress.
You don't speak with me the way the others
do, who tell me,
by green effort, by every half-drowning
and abdomen-push of new leaf,
they want to be trees,
trees tall enough to see over the trees.

You'll stay here and spread out, you say,
in a rumble of a voice
muffled by hair.
You are growing all up out of yourself!

Your roots are branches
so your leaves are the lawn!

If that's the way you are going to be—
deluxe, warm, a sexual fence
with the shapeliness of the many—
then you may have to be an entire nation
yourself,
just yourself in the center and also at the edges.

Who will want anything to do with you?
You get all over us.
You are an old man at heart.

I want to pity you,
freak among nations made up of individuals,
for you are an individual
composed of multitudes.

When a man wears a dress
or has so many legs,
it will always be noticed,
unless he is trying to pass for a tree.

Shoulders of Tropical Rain

It was plenty:
the heavy rain on my heavy shoulders
making them heavier—
and then nothing, no rain, no mist
(which is the shadow of rain),
no tear from a tree, no oily sparkle
on sidewalks, no rivulets
cutting the roads, no semblance, no truth
of rain, nothing.
And yet it rained here—here, hard, heavy,
swishing its wild damsel dresses,
bowing to nothing
but the curve of the earth, being
of its hundred thousand minds—
No, its trillion trillion times
trillion minds
for which the collecting word *rain*
is born of dim sight
and a grave curvature of belief
in angles and lines, collisions of fauna
and other instances of faith
that whatever happened will happen again.
What despair must have overtaken
the joy of those cold scientists
who studied the flakes of the snow
to learn that none were alike.
About drops of rain—
alike or unalike—we don't know.
And can't ask.
Rain survives only as rain,
while we, if the books are to be believed,
survive not only alive and awake,
but absent, expected, asleep or recently
departed. So bow down in the rain—

the force that all
but turns the wheel
which drives you into the ground.
For now it is on its way
on up again.

Unless It Was Courage

Again today, balloons aloft in the hazy *here*,
three heated, airy, basket-toting balloons,
three triangular boasts ahead against the haze
of summer and the gravity of onrushing fall—
these win me from the wavery *chrr*-ing of locusts
that fills these days the air between the trees,
from the three trembly outspreading cocoons hanging
on an oak so old it might have been weighed down
by the very thought of hundreds of new butterflies,
and from all other things that come in threes
or seem to be arranged. These *are* arranged,
they are the perfection of mathematics as idea,
they have lifted off by making the air greater—
nothing else was needed unless it was courage—
and today they do not even drag a shadow.

It was only a week ago I ran beneath one.
All month overhead had passed the jetliners,
the decorated company planes, the prop jobs
and great crows of greed and damage (I saw one
dangle a white snake from its bill as it flew),
and all month I had looked up from everywhere
to see what must seem from other galaxies
the flies of heaven. Then quickly my chance came,
and I ran foolish on the grass with my neck bent
to see straight up into the great resonant cavity
of one grandly wafting, rising, bulbous, whole
balloon, just to see nothing for myself. That
was enough, it seemed, as it ran skyward and away.
There I was, unable to say what I'd seen.
But I was happy, and my happiness made others happy.

To Be

How could I wake from childhood
when everywhere I went there was breathing
like a mother's breath at the ear of her child
before words; when in all places
there was touch and people who defied
the magazines, who did not look perfect and dead;
when my bodyguard was luck
and my texts were songs and the humming of the planets.

It was necessary that I hear a sizzle
in the lungs, and a hum on the wires. Fate decreed
that the magazines should multiply,
the child in me gradually decipher the air,
and the planets die. Fate, which is Kingdom Come,
called me out of the crowd
where I was shopping or doing some busywork,
and told me to stop singing and just be.

But I had an idea. Didn't the sun make it impossible
to look at the sun? Wasn't the night
known only by nuance, the darkness unstudied?
If I contained the earth and all of its flowers
but did not once look at them, would anyone know?
Thus, in my neighborhood, passion—even rapture!—
survived in secret, and still a child appears
in the guise of a grownup at dusk and story-time.

In Those Days

In those days, I was pulled as if by an undertow
from a far sea, and beauty; and hastening, fastening
my buttons as I went, I hurried to reach the delta
before a single wing took flight, and constantly
I was the black-robed trumpeter attending dawn,
playing into the brassy announcements of the sun
my Hindemith, my Haydn, my melancholy Voluntary.
And I was Taps and the muted echo of Taps.

All of this required a youthful half-stupor
through which I could make out many stone valleys
connected by corridors and windows. At each window:
voices without sound, a hook for my red jacket,
and a dreamy scene in the rain where back porches
were lit by candles. Phosphor in the paint on the ceiling
gave constellations their shine where they turned.
In reality, it was I who was turning; it was I at the window.

How did we find our way from the forced beginning
of each school day to the final bell? The daily miracle!
Someday, the bills will come due for the things we did
to save our souls—hundreds for writing on the walls,
for carving our names in the desks, this much
for a bad mouth, this much for sleeping in class. . . .
Something glazed our eyes and held our attention—
some mortar in the bloodstream, some blood in the cement.

The Facts of Life

This pebble never thought it would surface here
where I came walking to scuff it, wreck it, bother it,
and utterly transform it from a simple creature
of limited experience in the darkness of its mother
into a highly valued, polished star of daylight.
I, of course, was just passing the time by rolling it
back and forth under the sole of my shoe.

A psychiatrist would say I was worried at the time,
but I would say I was worried *all* of the time—
here with the trees taking sick and even the healthiest
rocking in the dirt from this disaster and that one,
so that bare plots of land where prairie grass shone
took up with tumult and history, forever locked,
and rocks appeared on cleared land without warning.

It's as if something in nature were asking my help,
but modestly, reluctantly, as politely as a black shoe.
I stood where I might see what was asked for,
by the dry sites of immense basements for new buildings
where pipe was being laid in the dusty man-made rivers
which run down everywhere beneath the deepest roots.
I stood and worked my foot back and forth like a rolling pin.

Out of the throat of the world, a pebble emerged.
And it said nothing, or was muffled before it could speak
by the innocence of bystanders, by the facts of life.
Dingy and shipwrecked, the buildings rose higher.
When the men broke from work under the threat of rain,
I took that star of daylight, my little marble,
into my hand, where it helped me to cut my way home.

Days of Time

Gone into the woods, they'll say, only because
I preferred the company of trees, any kind of tree,
to the company of . . . . It was a day like this one,
in the dark season, a time when one sits in the center
to avoid the flat wind that blows through the walls,
that time when icy vapors hover above the river
and the big pines move like old men in dark clothes
for an important occasion: the days of time, time of time.

Gone into the sea, they'll say, just because
I loved to walk on the darkened sand at the weed line
near to the scalloped edge of the ocean, and there
felt on the soles of my feet as the spent waves receded
the termites of ocean floors and the crab imprint
that gives the galaxy a picture of the galaxy.
It was a wide day in the sunshine, but narrow in the shadows,
when I walked around a bend in the beach and stayed.

Disappeared into thin air, they'll say, because
I stopped to look up at a giant red fan in the clouds
and a picture of four bakers peeking over the horizon,
and counted the wooden thread-spools in a cigar box.
It was a day like this one: sulphur hung in the air,
somewhere the earth vented the steam at its core.
It was a day in the future, just like this in the future,
when the melting wax no longer seemed to betray the candle.

Starfish

His entire body is but one hand, severed at the wrist. It lies on the sand in the late afternoon as if sunning itself. As he dries, he reaches ever more arthritically for the light itself with which to brown his palm. In this regard, his futility is unsurpassed.

You may pick him up now. Dead hand in your live hand. The mount of flesh just behind the thumb has been planed down and the soft tissue, tissue that will never tan, seems to have endured much scraping and dragging on the roughest edges of the sea, and to have fought back by raising its hackles, as it were, until it has become a hand of tiny spikes, but spikes nonetheless. Rub him in your palm, if you like. His hand is tougher than your own.

Of course, this starfish that we know is only the version run aground, becalmed, out of its element, preserved, petrified. In its lifetime, which we have missed entirely, it was soft, it was spongy, it was bread to the sea. Then, it molded itself to its element, water, not as a hand closes around a prized possession to become a fist, but as a wheel becomes motion without losing its shape even for a moment.

The starfish, alive, was a kind of wheel. The sea was its air, as all around us in what we call a universe are stars in space like fish in the ocean. Like fish, we know them only at a distance, we approach closer to them by means of glass and mirrors, we grow silent in the presence of the mysterious nature of them, we may only imagine touching them when they have been cast up on the beach or thrown down from light.

Such is our conception of Heaven, from which it seems we are forever finding souvenirs, signals, clues. We have no way of knowing whether, at any single moment, we are being led toward a Heaven that follows upon our lives or toward one that precedes it, or indeed whether or not these may be the same. Is it not then natural that we look down in the light and up in the darkness, and is it not also ironic that it requires a dark, absorbent object to stop our gaze in the former while it takes a moment of hard light to focus us in the latter? We shall never know the end of our thoughts, nor where they began.

Return to our starfish now. Time has given it a new, earthy odor.

In

In the earth, where there are stones, dimes, fingers.
In dirt, where there is soul and spirit.

In rain, in steps.
In sand, in fields of insects.

In fields of insects.
In victory-tailed swallows—

in the furious company of swallows where I walk
in the field, stirring insects, bargaining

in swallow-talk for company.
In victory-tailed swallow-talk as they eat.

In 1983. In Port Townsend, Wa.
In a mood to find the one tree, magic stone, pirate coin.

In the dark morning on wet sand with the gulls.
In the bright sky toward which we look to see

in death certain people we know who are gone.
In Dick Hugo, a child who wrote the poetry of a grownup.

In saying no more about it.
In asking neither praise nor blame in the name of mortality.

In living right here, where we find ourselves,
in who we are right now.

In who we are right now among the swallows eating insects
in a field, in pain from wanting too much.

In shade, then shadow. In life. In concert.
In the sign the swallows flash as they win the day.

The Nest

The day the birds were lifted from my shoulders,
the whole sky was blue, a long-imagined effect
had taken hold, and a small passenger plane
was beating the earth with its wings
as it swung over the bean fields toward home.
A fat car barely travelled a narrow road
while I waited at the bottom of a hill.
People around me were speaking loudly
but I heard only whispers, and stepped away.

You understand, I was given no choice.
For a long time, I was tired of whatever it was
that dug its way into my shoulders for balance
and whispered in my ears, and hung on for dear life
among tall narrow spaces in the woods
and in thickets and crowds, like those of success,
with whom one mingles at parties and in lecture halls.
In the beginning, there was this or that . . .
but always on my shoulders that which had landed.

That was life, and it went on in galleries
and shopping plazas, in museums and civic centers,
much like the life of any responsible man
schooled in the marriage of history and culture
and left to learn the rest at the legs of women.
In furtive rooms, in passing moments, the sea
reopened a door at its depth, trees spoke
from the wooden sides of houses, bodies became
again the nests in the naked tree.

After that, I was another person,
without knowing why or how, and after that,
I lived naked in a new world where the sun
broke through windows to grasp entire families

and crept between trees to wash down streets
without disturbing any object, in a world
where a solitary kiss blew down a door.
The day the birds were lifted from my shoulders,
it killed me—and almost cost me a life. . . .

MARVIN BELL

Marvin Bell was born August 3, 1937 in New York City and grew up in Center Moriches, on the south shore of eastern Long Island. He lives in Iowa City.